THE Lion AND THE Land OF Narnia

Illustrated & Compiled by

ROBERT CORDING

HARVEST HOUSE PUBLISHERS

EUGENE, OREGON

Dedication

For Edward and Ruth Cording

Friends and confidants in the Journey

Acknowledgments

Appreciation to C.S. Lewis, master of his art, and to Douglas Gresham for his continuing vision for the Narnian Chronicles. For each contributor to *The Lion and the Land of Narnia* who willingly shared their inspiring stories and unique impressions of Narnia, a heartfelt thanks. Special thanks and appreciation to Terry Glaspey for his editorial direction of *The Lion and the Land of Narnia* and for his ideas and insight from concept to completion. Thanks also to Kim Moore for her editing skills, Jeff Marion, Koechel Peterson & Associates for graphic design, and to Chris Mitchell and Marjorie Mead of the Marion Wade Center for their assistance in the project. For encouragement always from Ruth Cording (Mom), for interest and support from Margaret Cording Petty ("making the connection"), and Ed, Norma, and Evan Cording...thanks.

THE Lion AND THE Land OF Narnia

Text copyright © 2008 by Robert Cording

Artwork copyright © 2008 by Robert Cording and may not be reproduced without the artist's permission. For more information regarding art prints featured in this book, please contact Mr. Cording at www.robertcordingart.com. Poster size prints (18" x 24") of selected paintings and *giclee* canvas prints of all paintings are available.

Published by Harvest House Publishers
Eugene, Oregon 97402
www.harvesthousepublishers.com

ISBN-13: 978-0-7369-2037-7
ISBN-10: 0-7369-2037-4

Design and production by Koechel Peterson & Associates, Inc., Minneapolis, Minnesota

Harvest House Publishers has made every effort to trace the ownership of all poems and quotes. In the event of a question arising from the use of a poem or quote, we regret any error made and will be pleased to make the necessary correction in future editions of this book.

Extracts from various works & letters by C.S. Lewis,© C.S. Lewis Pte Ltd, are reprinted by permission.

"Not a Tame Lion," words and music by Carolyn Arends, © 2004 Running Arends Music (ASCAP). From the CD *Under the Gaze* (available at carolynarends.com).

Printed in Hong Kong

08 09 10 11 12 13 14 15 16 / NG / 10 9 8 7 6 5 4 3 2

Now we see in a mirror dimly, but then face to face;
now I know in part, but then I will know fully
just as I also have been fully known.

THE BOOK OF FIRST CORINTHIANS

THE Lion AND THE Land OF Narnia

A faun with an umbrella…standing in the snow holding parcels. This was an image conjured in the imagination of young Jack Lewis. Years later, more images and word pictures appeared: an old wardrobe, a lamppost on a snowy eve, the sound of sleigh bells, a gleaming castle above the sea, and a mysterious land where animals talk and fierce battles rage.

Then Aslan came bounding into his imagination; a great lion, magnificent and awesome. Thus Narnia was born in the creative mind of C.S. "Jack" Lewis. "I see pictures," he later wrote. "I have no idea whether this is the usual way of writing stories, still less whether it is the best. It is the only one I know: images always come first." From these images arose some of the greatest children's stories of our time.

Lewis was a storyteller even as a child. In a rambling three-story brick house on the out-skirts of rainy Belfast, Lewis and his brother, Warnie, conjured up stories about a land of dressed animals called Boxen. These creatures were a mixture of the kind of books the boys read (everything from *King Arthur* to *Gulliver's Travels*) and a child's understanding of the politics of the day.

Lewis's conversion to Christianity as a young Oxford don provided the seminal focus to which he could connect the great themes already in his imagination. As Ross Wilson has written, "C.S. Lewis did not just hang clothes in a wardrobe, he hung ideas—great ideas of sacrifice, redemption, victory, and freedom for the sons of Adam and the daughters of Eve…We should not stop looking. Some of the greatest things can be found in the most ordinary of places, like a wardrobe."

Lewis was the author of more than 60 books of literary scholarship, apologetics, practical theology, and fiction. Many of them have become modern classics. *Mere Christianity*, *The Screwtape Letters*, *The Four Loves*, and *The Problem of Pain* are among those that have inspired and delighted countless readers. But perhaps the most beloved are The Chronicles of Narnia, a series of fantasy stories cherished by young and old alike.

Somehow these are more than just stories to many of their readers. We are drawn into them and they become *our* stories. We cheer the thaw from the long winter to spring and see our reflection in the clear waters of Narnia. We identify with Peter, Susan, and Lucy, and share their hopes and fears, struggles and dreams. We know only too well our own failings and disappointments as we witness Edmund's folly. We fight the battles alongside them. And we encounter the majesty of Aslan.

For this book I have painted some of the things I have seen in Narnia, images brought to my own imagination from dramatic scenes in the land between the lamppost and the castle-by-the-sea.

And I have gathered together the thoughts of some people who have been inspired and influenced by the timeless stories of the Narnian Chronicles. Some are C.S. Lewis experts, some are children, some are passionate fans of the books—but they have all been moved to write about their own experiences and encounters in Aslan's world. I've also included some of Lewis's own thoughts on Narnia, taken from his correspondence.

I invite you to join with us as we journey just beyond the wardrobe and discover together the Lion and the Land of Narnia.

Robert Cording
Artist and Filmmaker

Douglas Gresham:
Growing Up in Narnia

Can you imagine what it must of have been like to have been a child who was hearing these stories even as they were being created?

That was the experience of Douglas Gresham, now an accomplished writer in his own right and Coproducer for the series of Narnia films. In a very real sense, Douglas can lay claim to having grown up in Narnia. His mother had read *The Lion, the Witch and the Wardrobe* aloud to him just after it was published, and it was his "very favorite book in the entire world." Then, at eight years old, his mother brought him along on a trip to England to meet her favorite writer. Imagine the excitement Douglas felt about getting to meet the man who had created the magical world of Narnia, one who was on speaking terms with King Peter and Aslan, the Great Lion. Douglas almost expected Lewis to be wearing armor and carrying a sword. Instead, he was introduced to a "stooped, balding, professorial gentleman with scruffy clothes and nicotine-stained fingers." Not at all what he had expected! But he was soon won over by Lewis's warmth, compassion, and incredible sense of humor.

When C.S. Lewis married Douglas's mother, the American writer Joy Davidman, he gained not only a special companion but also became a stepfather to two young boys: David and Douglas. Joy brought much happiness to Lewis's life, but her untimely death left her sons in the care of Lewis and his brother, Warren.

Not only would Lewis read aloud to Douglas passages of the books as he was writing them, but it was not uncommon for mealtime conversation to light upon such topics as the culinary preferences of Narnian dwarfs or the latest unrecorded exploits of such characters as Puddleglum, Reepicheep, and the heroic Lucy Pevensie.

For Douglas, sometimes Narnia seemed every bit as real as the world around him. And as each new book was released, he was among the very first to explore the latest adventures of the Narnian Chronicles. Today, through his vision of bringing Narnia (and Aslan) to life in the cinema, these timeless stories of C.S. Lewis live on.

Tumnus

Stories About Hope

I once was a little boy who believed that most animals could speak but chose not to, and that hovering above me was a cozy world presided over by a pandalike king, whose favorite toy was the moon and whose greatest joy was to share it, especially with me as I lay abed in the dark. I could not explain these beliefs then and have never cared to since. My imagination had spoken.

Fifteen years thereafter, during a graduate school summer of 1968, eating badly, sleeping worse, and losing weight, I was blessed with the worst cold I have ever had. Now—and in good conscience—I could actually stop working. A dark, heavy rain fell steadily, insulating me in my seclusion as I lay close by an open window enjoying my favorite weather. Although a lifelong reader of faerie, I had somehow put off reading the Chronicles, which just now seemed perfectly suited to the circumstances. So for five days I read the seven books, drinking in all of their danger, heroism, and merriment, which both quenched and aroused a great thirst. I had never before been taken so utterly out of myself to that reality-right-around-the-corner, a reality perpetually new, awful, rampant, true, and good.

Needless to say I have believed them the 40 years since. For they invite me to wonder, *So that's how the Old Testament and the Gospels work,* and I read Scripture afresh as the greatest wonder tales ever written. And I think further, *So that's how this world and I are made, to point to and to be called by the next, where, like Lucy, I belong.* The dynamic is straightforward: Desire summons the cardinal virtue of hope. The Chronicles are more than anything else about hope—*the exalted and continual conveyance of which is C.S. Lewis's greatest achievement.* And that is why The Chronicles of Narnia never fail to break my heart.

James Como
Author of *C.S. Lewis at the Breakfast Table*

14 September 1957

Dear Lucy,

I am so glad you like the Narnian stories and it was nice of you to write and tell me. I love E. Nesbit too and I think I have learned a lot from her about how to write stories of this kind. Do you know Tolkein's The Lord of the Rings? I think you would like it. I am also bad at Maths and it is a continual nuisance to me—I get muddled over my change in shops. I hope you'll have better luck and get over the difficulty! It makes life a lot easier.

It makes me, I think, more humble than proud to know that Aslan has allowed me to be the means of making Him more real to you. Because He could have used anyone—as He made a donkey preach a good sermon to Balaam.

Perhaps, in return, you will sometime say a prayer for me?

With all good wishes,

Yours sincerely,

C. S. Lewis

Narnia is a wonderful reminder that childlike faith is real. That I am not silly for wanting to run around and tell everyone I meet that the characters of the Bible—the kings and queens, the princes and paupers, and of course, the Jesus-man—are all more real than any of us can ever imagine. That crossing through a wardrobe door of decision launches us into one of the greatest adventures possible.

Margaret Feinberg
Author of *The Organic God*

"When they tried to look at Aslan's face they just caught a glimpse of the
golden mane and the great, royal, solemn, overwhelming eyes...
Peter...advanced to the Lion and said, 'We have come—Aslan.'"

C.S. Lewis, *The Lion, the Witch and the Wardrobe*

Lewis's character Aslan has helped shape my perception of God, for it is certainly Jesus Christ that C.S. Lewis portrayed through this beloved lion. I decided to become a Christian when I was very young, but my understanding of my Creator is constantly growing. Aslan helped me visualize how God could be merciful, just, loving, and frightening all at the same time. In famous lines from *The Lion, the Witch and the Wardrobe*, Mr. Beaver says, "Of course he isn't safe. But he is good. He's the King, I tell you." He later states, "He's wild, you know. Not like a *tame* lion." Aslan is a snapshot of Lewis's view of God, and it has helped me in mine.

Anne Kyle, age 14

I thought Narnia was really cool. The boy got into trouble with his sisters and his brother for playing games and leaving with the Ice Princess, but he was just joking and went back to them. I really liked the reindeer best.

Ethan Derosiers, age 5

Narnia is the classic battle between good and evil. *The Lion, the Witch and the Wardrobe* gives a good picture of Jesus dying on the cross. Aslan was the perfect character to represent Jesus in the story. I like Narnia because of the action and adventure of the story and because it also tells people about the story of Jesus in another way.

Matthew White, age 11

More Than Children's Stories

The Chronicles of Narnia have never been children's stories to me. I first read them at the age of 19, just after my first year of college. I was still very new to the Christian faith, having met the Lord as a senior in high school. Some dear believers who would never steer me wrong recommended I read these stories and gave me a pretty little boxed set. I put off reading the books for months as I finished a difficult first year as a biology student.

Soon after school ended I had to get on a plane to Alaska to visit a relative. I threw the whole box of books in my carry-on backpack because I was in a panic to get to the airport. And then there I was, stuck on a plane trip that would take about eight hours. I broke open the set and started to read.

I was totally transported. In terms of competing for my attention, the grand mountain vistas passing by outside on a clear day were simply no match for the new worlds that were opening up in those amazing stories. Not only were the characters and plots creative and riveting, but C.S. Lewis opened my eyes to the idea that the magnificent themes of the gospel were timeless, boundless, and utterly captivating.

Craig J. Hazen

Professor of Christian Apologetics,
Biola University

Re-enchantment

Narnia brings to mind, first and foremost, the notion of enchantment, or better yet, of re-enchantment. What I have found most meaningful is Narnia's ability to recover the wonder of the ordinary and permanent things of life. Creative fantasy, of which Narnia participates, is about regaining a clear view of things, of seeing things as we were meant to see them.

G.K. Chesterton said that such tales tell us "apples were golden only to refresh the forgotten moment when we found that they were green. They make rivers run with wine only to make us remember, for one wild moment, that they run with water." Similarly, J.R.R. Tolkien observed that in fairy stories we meet "the centaur and the dragon" with the hope that we come away beholding "sheep, and dogs, and horses—and wolves" as things more remarkable than either centaurs or dragons, for the former are real and the latter are not. The recovery of the truly enchanted nature of our world is what fairy stories help us do. This is ultimately what Narnia means to me—with each new reading it succeeds in liberating the world of the everyday from the "drab triteness" of the familiar, opening my eyes once again to the reality of the truly extraordinary nature of the wonders that surround me and breathing into each new day a freshness that more often than not leads me to praise the One who has made it all.

Christopher Mitchell
Director of the Wade Center, Wheaton College

A Young Correspondent

My first encounter with Narnia was in 1957 in a battered green bookmobile, which served our newly minted suburb in lieu of a real library. Arriving every Wednesday in the parking lot of an equally newly minted phenomenon, the strip mall, I would climb aboard the converted bus looking for another world in the long shelves running down each side. Even at the advanced age of seven, the experience of what Lewis would later teach me to call "Sehnsucht," or unappeasable longing, dictated my reading choices. I wanted adventure, fantasy, fairy tales, science fiction; anything which pointed to something more than the world I lived in could give me.

I don't remember much about that first reading of *The Lion, the Witch and the Wardrobe* except that I liked it sufficiently to request it again a few years later from the librarian/driver of the bookmobile. I didn't even remember the full title, just that it was about a Lion and a Witch. This time through I paid more attention, and I noticed that there was a sequel, *Prince Caspian*. After that I kept a sharp watch for anything by C.S. Lewis.

By now, as a mature 12-year-old, I had begun corresponding with Lewis, who was gracious enough to answer my letters. Because I was accompanying my English neighbor to England in April of 1964 as babysitter to her two-year-old, I made plans to visit Lewis in Oxford. I received my last letter from him, dated November 11, 1963, so I didn't know that he had died just 11 days later until seeing an article in *The Saturday Evening Post* ascribed to the "late" C.S. Lewis. My trip to England took place anyway, and my hosts were gracious enough to take me to Headington Quarry for my birthday, where Lewis's brother, Warnie, showed us around and allowed me to press flowers out of the garden.

None of this seemed remarkable except in retrospect. As I did my college thesis on Lewis's view of mythopoeic language, I came to understand the largeness of his intellect and the breadth of his ability, far beyond being my personal guide to finding Aslan and Aslan's true meaning.

The trickiest thing for me was to make the transition from Aslan to Jesus. Oh, I saw what Lewis was getting at, but it took a long while before I could really believe that the warm and vital Aslan bore any real connection to the flat and pallid Jesus I had encountered in Sunday school. And there lies Lewis's genius. He uses story, as did his friend Tolkien, to "fly under the radar" of our prejudices and mistaken notions. Although Lewis never set out to write an evangelistic tract in The Chronicles of Narnia, nevertheless, his story pointed me to the true Story, as it must have done for many others. And I will hope for many more.

Kathy Keller

Redeemer Presbyterian Church

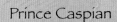

Prince Caspian

Lifetime Stories

I had never heard of C.S. Lewis until my first year of college. I read his science fiction trilogy first and then *Mere Christianity*. After that I devoured just about every book I could get my hands on by C.S. Lewis—except the Narnian Chronicles. At the ripe old age of 19, I felt I just didn't have time for "bedtime stories."

Finally one summer I decided to dip into the first few pages of *The Lion, the Witch and the Wardrobe* to see if there was anything there to hold my interest. I read the whole book in two days. In the next two weeks, I went on to read all seven books in the Chronicles. I quickly learned that these "bedtime stories" were also "lifetime stories," books I have returned to over and over again throughout the years. Lewis himself would have understood perfectly the revolution in my reading. "When I became a man," he explained, "I put away childish things, including the fear of childishness and the desire to be very grown up."

Paradoxically, Lewis's stories for children are also the products of his maturity. Though he was writing what he considered "holiday fiction," Lewis poured his whole self into the Chronicles—his mellow spirituality, his love of wonder and enchantment, his affection for animals and homespun things, and his shrewd observations about human nature. Each Narnia book is like a little wardrobe. It contains a looking glass in which readers will see themselves in surprising new ways. And each time they turn the pages, they will enter again into a visionary world of bustling vitality, moral clarity, and sparkling beauty.

David C. Downing
Professor of English and author of *Into the Wardrobe*

A Threshold

C.S. Lewis's wardrobe fascinates me. It is a boundary separating dissimilar worlds. That's what thresholds do.

Bent against a bitter wind, a traveler steps over a cabin threshold and he's warm and safe.

A civilian crosses a gangway threshold and he's off to war.

Three children enter a wardrobe and they're in Narnia, where animals talk and adventures abound, where boys are kings and girls are queens.

We cross thresholds every day. Not all are magical. Some serve merely to divide our lives into manageable compartments. In time there is one threshold everyone must cross, the one separating this life from the next. As Christians we need not fear the crossing. Imagine death as a wardrobe threshold. On the other side awaits adventure, self-realization, and a lion king.

Jack Cavanaugh
Novelist

A Glimpse of Heaven

Narnia, an imaginative creation of heartbreaking beauty, evokes a longing in me for the eternal. In that magical world I encounter the Creator, Savior, and King of Kings in Aslan. With Lucy, I can ride on his back and frolic; with Aravis, I am chased and chastened by Him; with Jill, I am carried on His warm, sweet breath or sense His protective presence even in the deepest, darkest caverns. In Narnia my imagination enables me to comprehend more clearly how Jesus, my Savior and Lord, is also my Deliverer, Protector, and Friend. For me the Wardrobe door opens into the magical realm of the imagination and the mystical realm of the eternal.

In Narnia I can catch a glimpse of heaven.

Melanie M. Jeschke
Author of The Oxford Chronicles

Extraordinary in the Midst of the Ordinary

There are moments in life when we are touched by the sense of the other—the unknown, the extraordinary—in the midst of the ordinary. Such is the case when the Pevensie children hear the name of Aslan for the first time. They sense the import of the name of Aslan, even though they have never heard it before. They know that it has meaning just as if they had experienced the true meaning of the name in a dream long ago. This sense of awe and mystery and the ordinary yet extraordinary pervades of *The Lion, the Witch and the Wardrobe*.

In each of our lives, there are moments that are pregnant with meaning when we are able to sense but not quite decipher. These are the moments when knowledge of God and His grace are close to us. They are, in a sense, obtuse moments because if we look directly at them, the meaning disappears. It is important at those times to listen without trying to interpret, to let God speak to you without trying to shape what He says to your will.

Ted Baehr and **Peirce Baehr**
Movieguide Ministry

The Word and the Lion

Jesus Christ was the centre of C.S. Lewis's life, and it should not surprise us that his greatest literary achievement is Aslan. "Aslan," Lewis explained, "is an invention giving an imaginary answer to the question, 'What might Christ become like if there really were a world like Narnia and He chose to be incarnate and die and rise again in *that* world as He actually has done in ours?'" This means that, instead of imagining the incarnate Jesus of Nazareth reappearing in Narnia as a Lion, we are to imagine the eternal Son of God coming straight down from heaven to Narnia and becoming incarnate there as a Lion.

There are, of course, similarities because Jesus is the Son of God and Aslan is a portrayal of the same character. However, by having the Son of God experience life in a world of animals, Lewis wanted to show us what He might be like in a totally different mode of existence.

To appreciate the greatness of Lewis's accomplishment we should notice three things: (1) At no point does Aslan do or say anything that contradicts what Jesus did or said. I believe that if you mixed up a dozen sayings of Christ with a dozen sayings of Aslan, those who are not biblical scholars could not easily tell who said what. And if you mistook a saying of Aslan for a saying of Jesus, what harm would it do? (2) In many instances what happens to Aslan in Narnia illuminates the experiences of our Lord in this world. The obvious example is Aslan's death on the Stone Table. Those who are deeply moved by it will, when they go back to the Bible, be more deeply moved by the crucifixion, seeing it in a new light.

And (3) because the Scriptures include only a fraction of what Jesus said, Lewis attempted to "fill in the gaps," so to speak, by having Aslan do and say what Christ might have done and said. Probably because he was asked if Jesus ever said anything funny, Lewis fills the Narnian stories with humor. A delightful example occurs in *The Magician's Nephew* where, after the Jackdaw makes a joke, he says: "Aslan! Aslan! Have I made the first joke? Will everybody always be told how I made the first joke?" "You have only *been* the First Joke." And who could forget how, in *The Horse and His Boy,* Aslan turns the pompous Rabadash into an ass?

Walter Hooper

Author and former personal
secretary to C.S. Lewis

Shadows of Another World

There are thin places in the walls of the universe where we go to see the shadows of another world. There, the sounds, smells, and sights of distant shores twist and bend, making their way through time and space to squeeze through the thinness and pierce through our puny senses.

However distorted our vision, we know that home is somewhere else as well as here. So we go to the thin places. We long for the faintest scent of that other place. Our ears strain for the roar of a lion and the crack of a broken table. We hunger for a taste of glory.

Somehow the back of a wardrobe must give way, providing passage to the land of our heart.

Dan Scott

Author of *Naked and Not Ashamed*

"The rising sun had made everything look so different...
The Stone Table was broken into two pieces by a great crack that
ran down it from end to end. There, shining in the sunrise, larger
than they had seen him before...stood Aslan himself."

C.S. Lewis, *The Lion, the Witch and the Wardrobe*

Awakening to Life

I first became aware of the writings of C.S. Lewis when my children were reading *The Screwtape Letters* and *Out of the Silent Planet* in school.

Then we discovered *The Lion, the Witch and the Wardrobe* and fell in love with Narnia and the Chronicles. Lewis gave us a gift. A breathtaking journey into a world of enchantment, into a land of mystery. There were doors one could go through by magic, and mystical creatures and animals that could think and reason.

Above all there was Aslan, the lion, who said to the girl Jill, "You would not have called to me unless I had been calling you."

Scene by scene and around every corner was wonder and anticipation. The stories inspired us to see hidden truths and traces of the "deep magic" in our own world.

From the lamppost to Cair Paravel, we followed the children through Narnia.

One of our favorite scenes was of Susan and Lucy riding with Aslan on the way to the witch's castle.

We were captivated by the "picture" of the great lion soaring over the wall into the courtyard and spellbound as the stone statues came to life. C.S. Lewis once wrote of this scene: "This is precisely what Christianity is about. This world is a great sculptor's shop. We are the statues, and there is a rumor going round the shop that some of us are someday going to come to life."

Ruth Cording
Author of *C. S. Lewis: A Celebration of His Early Life*

Aslan Is on the Move!

I first read the Narnian books when was I was a senior in high school. Since that initial literary encounter, I have reread each one of the seven volumes numerous times—too numerous to count. But the most memorable of all of these experiences is the time I first read *The Lion, the Witch and the Wardrobe* to my son, Ryan.

I began reading to Ryan when he was just six months old, as soon as he could sit upright on my lap. We started with picture books, and though the text might have been beyond his comprehension at certain points, he loved listening to the words and looking at the various illustrations. Before long I had only to pick up a book that he recognized as belonging to him, and he would race to my side—always ready to hear a story.

The bookcases in his room were filled to overflowing with all sorts of books, many from my own childhood days—and very often books which I continued to read and enjoy as an adult. Among these volumes were The Chronicles of Narnia.

One day when he was three years old, Ryan discovered *The Lion, the Witch and the Wardrobe* on his bedroom bookshelf and asked to have the story read to him. He was greatly intrigued by the book cover, and it soon became clear that it would be easier to comply than to dissuade him from his choice. And so, without context or discussion, I began to read the book aloud to him, assuming that as a young toddler, he would quickly grow bored with the advanced story.

continued >>

But, in fact, Ryan was thoroughly captivated, and it was only at my request, after having read through several chapters together, that we finally took a break. This pattern of reading continued over the next few days until one evening, after having just listened to chapter 7, Ryan sidled up to a dinner guest (fortunately a high school English teacher who knew and loved the Narnian tales) and in a whisper confided: "Have you heard? Aslan is on the move!"

I often use this true-life example in my own teaching on the Narnian tales as a means to illustrate the power of story. Three-year-old Ryan did not come to *The Lion, the Witch and the Wardrobe* with any advance preparation about the tale he was to hear. Nor was he already aware of the identity of the Great Lion, Aslan, or even of the various ways in which Aslan embodies elements from the life of Christ. All Ryan knew was that this story was exciting and that he longed to hear it unfold. As a result, his response to the character of Aslan was made on the intuitive level, as he responded to the story with his imaginative heart.

And, indeed, this is the very way that Lewis wanted his readers to experience the mythic fantasy that he created in The Chronicles of Narnia. When the name of Aslan is first heard by the Pevensie children in *The Lion, the Witch and the Wardrobe,* they respond with a sense of wonder and awe—a numinous sense that my child imaginatively echoed when he listened to the story.

Marjorie Mead
The Wade Center, Wheaton College

"They found themselves in the middle of a stone court-yard full of statues. Then Aslan breathed on them... The sight they saw was so wonderful...Everywhere the statues were coming to life... 'Aslan! Aslan! I've found Mr. Tumnus.'...A moment later Lucy and the little Faun...were dancing round and round for joy."

C.S. Lewis, *The Lion, the Witch and the Wardrobe*

Narnia is a world trapped inside another world. The story has wonderful excitement. I like the excitement because the characters fight in battles. The lion is a King. He is very big and controls everything in his world. He can also talk. Everyone obeys the lion when he gives commands to people or animals. I also think it is interesting because most of the characters get along, and that is hard for brothers and sisters to do sometimes. All in all, I like this story because the brothers and sisters work together to get out of danger when they are put into a world of wonderment.

Rose K. Givan, age 10

My mom read *The Lion, the Witch and the Wardrobe* to me when I was in first grade. There was something about the combination of magic, swordplay, fantasy, adventure, and creativity of Lewis's books that I was and still am enthralled with. Narnia was more than just an elementary pastime; it continues to intrigue me as I come to understand the symbols, themes, and moral maxims embedded in the books. I long to go "further up and further in" to Lewis's books, not only to relive childhood fantasy, but also to uncover those themes, symbols, and morals that I may have missed or only faintly grasped at an earlier age. However, I hope never to become "too old" for his books. One of my favorite things about reading the Chronicles was those moments when Lewis would take you aside and tell you something that only kids could really understand, something beyond the comprehension of silly grown-ups who had become "too old." The imagination became our "ring" that took us to the wood between the worlds or the magic that whisked us back to Narnia. Such is the wonderful imagination of his books.

Christopher Kyle, age 16

The Kilns, Kiln Lane
Headington Quarry
Oxford

21st November 1963

Dear Phillip,

To begin with, may I congratulate you on writing such a remarkably good letter; I certainly
could not have written it at your age. And to
go on with, thank you for telling me that you
like my books, a thing an author is always
pleased to hear. It is a funny thing that all
the children who have written to me see at once
who Aslan is, and grown-ups *never* do!

I haven't myself read the Puffin reprint you refer
to, so of course missed the fault; but I will
call the publisher's attention to it.

Please tell your father and mother [how] glad I
am to hear that they find my serious books of
some value.

With all best wishes to you and to them,

Yours sincerely,

C. S. Lewis

(**Editor's Note:** On Friday, November 22, 1963, the day after this
letter was typed, C.S. Lewis died peacefully at his home, The Kilns.
His sixty-fifth birthday would have been the following week.)

In The Chronicles of Narnia, C.S. Lewis paints a vivid picture of a wild and magical country. When describing it, many would depict a snow-covered wonderland or recount the intriguing animals found there, but what really draws me to Narnia is not what is seen on the outside. It's not creatures or culture. What draws me to Narnia is the reflection of my own life and struggles. It parallels many of my own thoughts and feelings—the need for something more, the call to come home, and the ultimate victory which Christ had over death. Narnia not only plays out the struggles that are paramount in our lives, but it also gives each one of us a hope and a deeper understanding of them. When C.S. Lewis first began writing The Chronicles of Narnia, there was great opposition to fantasy, saying that children needed books that helped them relate to reality. But The Chronicles of Narnia proved just the opposite. By using fantasy to depict real-life struggles, Lewis helps us to better understand ourselves. Narnia has deeply impacted many individuals' lives, including my own, by giving me word pictures that I can ponder.

Nathan White, age 14

The Apologetics of Narnia

I first discovered Narnia in the basement of my parents' friends' house two miles from Mendenhall Glacier near Juneau, Alaska. Neither Alaska nor Narnia have quite left me since: enriching my life even in slums outside Bombay, exhaust-choked Chinese cities, or sordid districts in Taiwan.

A friend in Hong Kong used to call me "Puddleglum," no doubt for my cheery disposition, and mingled my name with the tribe of Marsh-wiggles. Maybe I took her jokes as a calling. Ever since, I've wandered through an Underland of skepticism, Marxism, Buddhism, and Gnostic philosophy with a mission parallel to that of my webfooted mentor: to lead captives out of intellectual gloom and into the light of Christ. The Chronicles of Narnia are wonderful training for a Christian apologist.

The books are sneaky. You think you're reading children's tales about talking mice, fauns, and centaurs? You think Lewis is a little sloppy, the way he mixes his mythologies? Watch out! A profound view of life and ideas of how to

Puddleglum

think critically wait like Susan with her bow to ambush you. Is faith just wishful thinking? Puddleglum's speech in Underland is a brilliant response to deconstructionist views of life. Why should we believe the Christian God over other religions? Aslan's "I was the lion" speech to Shasta and his welcome to Emeth reflect subtle Christian teaching on the "divine logos," or what Justin Martyr called "tutors to Christ" in other faiths. Can we believe the remarkable claims Jesus makes about Himself? "There are only three possibilities," the professor reminds us, yet his logic represents not a narrowing, like the arguments of a Dawkins or Harris, but a broadening of possibilities of what it means to be human, backed up by the latest and best scholarship on the historical Jesus. The whole gang—Monopods, Reepicheep, and, of course, Puddleglum—follow me into my own books, where they always have helpful things to say.

David Marshall
Author of *The Truth Behind the New Atheism*

Reepicheep

The Planets and Narnia

It was nearly midnight and I was lying in bed, reading, when I made the discovery. I was reading two things at once. In one hand I had the chapter on the medieval view of the heavens from Lewis's *The Discarded Image*. In the other hand I had his 1935 poem on the self-same subject of medieval cosmology, entitled "The Planets." I was wanting to compare Lewis's academic approach to the seven planets—which give us the names of the days of the week—with his imaginative expression of them in his poetry.

It was when I read the poem's lines about Jupiter that I did a double take. The influence of Jupiter (or Jove), Lewis wrote, brings about "winter passed and guilt forgiven." *Hmm, I thought, that's rather like what goes on in* The Lion, the Witch and the Wardrobe, *isn't it? The White Witch's winter passes and Edmund's guilt is forgiven.* I read on. Jove, the poem told me, inspires "the lion-hearted" (*hmm, like Aslan, and that other, lesser lion in the same book*). Jove gives rise to "jocund revel/Laughter of ladies" (*like Aslan's resurrection romp with Susan and Lucy*). Jove's children are "just and gentle" (*like King Edmund the Just and Queen Susan the Gentle*). By now I was beginning to wake up a bit.

continued >>

"In the darkness something was happening... A voice had begun to sing. Then... the blackness overhead, all at once, was blazing with stars... a thousand, thousand points of light leaped out—single stars, constellations, and planets, brighter and bigger than any in our world."

C.S. Lewis, *The Magician's Nephew*

The more I looked at what Lewis wrote about Jupiter, the more I seemed to be reading a sort of plot summary of his first Narnia Chronicle. Jupiter's chief quality was "kingliness," and I recalled the first description of Aslan: "He's the King of the wood…the King of Beasts…He's the King, I tell you." Then I remembered how the story was essentially a conflict between Edmund and Peter about two different kinds of sovereignty. Edmund is tempted by the Witch with a false promise of kingship ("I want a nice boy…who would be King of Narnia when I am gone"). Peter, in contrast, is shown by Aslan the castle of Cair Paravel "where you are to be King…you will be High King over all the rest." "The rest" includes Edmund, for, of course, Edmund is restored to his *true* destiny by the Christlike death and resurrection of the King of the Beasts.

Lewis once wrote that, symbolically speaking, "the huge reddish spot which astronomers observe on the surface of Jupiter is a wound and the redness is that of blood. Jupiter, the planet of kingship, thus wounded becomes…another enctype [copy] of the Divine King wounded on Calvary."

Could I really have stumbled on a hidden theme? I was still in some doubt, but then two things clinched it. I turned to Lewis's introduction to the poem. There he wrote, "The characters of the planets…seem to me to have a permanent value as spiritual symbols… which is specially worth while in our own generation. Of Saturn we know more than enough. But who does not need to be reminded of Jove?"

Then I got out of bed to thumb through *The Lion, the Witch and the Wardrobe,* and I found that almost the first thing Peter says when he walks through the wardrobe into Narnia is, "By Jove!"

And *then* I wondered whether the other six Chronicles were also linked to the planets. As I stood there, in my pajamas, very wide awake indeed by this stage, I saw that this was so. *Prince Caspian* was the Mars story, *The Voyage of the Dawn Treader* the Sun, *The Silver Chair* the Moon, *The Horse and His Boy* was Mercury, *The Magician's Nephew* Venus, and *The Last Battle* Saturn. Good heavens!

Since that memorable night in February 2003, I have reread everything Lewis ever wrote, and I am in no doubt that he used these "spiritual symbols" to provide the imaginative theme of each Chronicle. He kept quiet about the theme because it was his belief that stories work best when they silently communicate a literary atmosphere, which he called "the kappa element in romance." *Kappa* is the initial letter of the Greek word *krypton,* meaning "hidden" or "cryptic." The planetary symbolism cryptically accounts for the major events of each tale, countless points of ornamental details, and, most importantly, the way that Aslan, the divine lion, is depicted.

It's a beautiful and artistic thing that Lewis did, putting his medieval expertise at the service of his Christian imagination. I hope now that the secret has at last come to light it will send readers back to the Chronicles with a renewed interest in their multilayeredness and a greater understanding of the skill with which they were composed.

Michael Ward
Author of *Planet Narnia: The Seven Heavens in the Imagination of C.S. Lewis*

The Dreamer and the Realist

Narnia is a place created for both the dreamer and the realist. The dreamer longs for its vastness, beauty, and landmarks that plant meaning, wonder, and awe in the landscape of the soul. An open wardrobe, a wooded glen, a lamppost amid fir trees dusted with snow, and hills beyond leading to adventure. Yes, we dream, ever longing to see Aslan bounding full speed across the Narnian horizon, coming for us, coming to take us home. But for the realist Narnia is much more than a story of a mythical land only found in the imagination. For now we live in the Shadowlands and Narnia reminds us of a land ahead without shadows, where the Son has risen and His light will forever quench the winter darkness. For me Narnia is a place of refuge, a world I visited often during my wife's struggle with cancer. And it is a constant reminder of a world yet to come. More than fantasy, it touches and embraces the longing we were born with that will be satisfied at the end of all things.

Throughout my life I have held tightly to the Lion's mane, not quite knowing where we're going, but trusting the One who carries me. "Further up and further in" is not mere wishful thinking but the heart of the gospel. The great promise of our King and Lord was of His return to take us to our real home, to be with Him forever reunited with loved ones lost here but found there. Somehow, in visiting Narnia I sense the very presence of God echoing through its canyons, carried along by its streams, and reflected upon its mountains. In this high country I discovered the goodness of God, the peace that He promised, and the hope He gave His life for. The dream and reality will join and take flight, and finally we'll experience joy unspeakable. So I listen for Aslan's roar, I anticipate His promised return, and I am thankful for my many journeys to Narnia, a pale reflection of heaven. We cannot comprehend what awaits us, but soon we will be there together. Until then enter the wardrobe, enjoy the scenery, and be on your way...Aslan is waiting.

Darren Jacobs
Screenwriter

Not a Tame Lion

I adored the Narnia stories as a child, but it wasn't until I was well into my twenties that I realized how much the image of Aslan could help me understand my own tendency to domesticate God. When I've found myself grappling with the aspects of God that frighten me or defy my understanding, I remember what Mr. Beaver told the Narnian children: "Who said anything about safe? 'Course he isn't safe. But he's good. He's the King, I tell you." Lewis, more than any other writer, has helped me to acknowledge and even celebrate the otherness and awesomeness and even fearsomeness of our very great God (Romans 11:33-36).

"Not a Tame Lion"

You're not a tame lion
You're not meek and mild
Your tenderness is reckless
And your mercy's wild
You're not a lucky rabbit's foot
And you're not Santa Claus
There is a certain fury to the love of God
You're not a tame lion

Caroyln Arends

Author, singer, songwriter

My Real Country

There have been times in my life when I yearned for the breathtaking beauty and justice of heaven. Then there have been others where the glory of earth—marrying my husband, birthing my children, talking long and deep with a friend—are so brimming with life that I don't want to leave. In *The Last Battle,* Lewis salves my conundrum with these words from the Unicorn: "I have come home at last! This is my real country! I belong here. This is the land I have been looking for all my life, though I never knew it until now. The reason why we loved the old Narnia is that it sometimes looked a little like this."

What is amazing and compelling on this earth is just a snapshot of the glory to come, so I wait on tiptoes.

Mary DeMuth
Novelist

Table Talk

My first genuine encounter with the Narnian Chronicles came in the late 1970s. I did not actually read the books—I *heard* them. Although audio books were not readily available in those days, my wife, Mary, has always loved to read aloud. Therefore, for several months she sipped coffee and read a daily chapter to me and our two children. Ten-year-old Michael, four-year-old Erika, and I ate breakfast with our attention riveted to these enthralling stories about several English children who climbed into an old wardrobe, only to find themselves stepping out into an enchanting land called Narnia. Talking beavers, a hospitable faun, a wicked witch, and a host of other characters all lived their lives in fierce opposition to or with courageous loyalty to an awesome and powerful lion called Aslan.

There is no way to measure the impact of C.S. Lewis's powerful works of imagination on our family. Nevertheless, I can say with certainty that these books profoundly touched all of our souls. In those days I was either a very new convert to the Christian faith or else just teetering on the brink of becoming one. In either case, my good wife's desire to introduce the family to C.S. Lewis helped launch me on a lifelong endeavor to learn all that I could from Lewis's writings, and eventually to write and edit several books and articles about his life and spiritual formation. In brief, this encounter with Narnia more than three decades ago caused me to make a career change and become an ordained minister of the gospel of Jesus Christ. Furthermore, Mary's soul received rich nourishment from Lewis's books, and her breakfast table readings played no small role in helping both of our children become committed Christians.

Lyle W. Dorsett
Author of *Seeking the Secret Place:
The Spiritual Formation of C.S. Lewis*

A Happy Ending

I vividly remember the first time I read The Chronicles of Narnia. Somehow my elementary school education was lacking, and so I found myself reading these books as an adult. Each evening before bedtime, I cuddled up with my seven-year-old son, David, on the sofa, and we read through the amazing and wonderful books that comprise the Chronicles. I remember the sense of adventure and new horizons the books brought to our imagination. We couldn't wait for our story time to begin each evening.

As we reluctantly neared the end of *The Last Battle,* I remember my eyes filled up with tears and my voice began to waiver as I tried to read the last page. My son looked up at me and said, "Mom, why are you crying? This book has a happy ending." Looking back, I think that is probably why I was crying. Narnia, like our life, has a cover and a title page, and like Peter, Edmund, Susan, and Lucy we too will one day begin *Chapter 1 of the Great Story…which goes on forever; in which every chapter is better than the one before.* My son was right. We can have a Happy Ending.

Donna Nuss
Campus Ministry Associate

The Dawn Treader

June 3rd 1953

Dear Hila,

Thank you so much for your lovely letter and pictures. I realized at once that the coloured one was not a particular scene but a sort of line-up like what you would have at the very end if it was a play instead of stories. *The Voyage of the "Dawn Treader"* is *not* to be last: There are to be 4 more, 7 in all. Didn't you notice that Aslan said nothing about Eustace not going back? I thought the best of your pictures was the one of Mr. Tumnus at the bottom of the letter. As to Aslan's other name, well I want you to guess. Has there never been anyone in this world who (1.) Arrived at the same time as Father Christmas. (2.) Said he was the son of the Great Emperor. (3.) Gave himself up for someone else's fault to be jeered at and killed by wicked people. (4.) Came to life again. (5.) Is sometimes spoken of as a Lamb (see the end of the *Dawn Treader*). Don't you really know His name in this world? Think it over and let me know your answer!

Reepicheep in your coloured picture has just the right perky, cheeky expression. I love real mice. There are lots in my rooms in College but I have never set a trap. When I sit up late working they poke their heads out from behind the curtains just as if they were saying, "Hi! Time for *you* to go to bed. We want to come out and play."

All good wishes,

Yours ever,

C. S. Lewis

Drawn into the Magic

I first became aware of Narnia when I was 14 years old. It was the summer between tenth and eleventh grades, and I was wandering through garage sales looking for some fun summer reading. A lady recommended a boxed set of books titled The Chronicles of Narnia. They looked a bit young to me, but with a shrug of my teen shoulders I thought I would give them a chance.

I was drawn into the magic almost by the first words. What a lovely introduction to the well of literary wisdom and Christian theology of C.S. Lewis. Narnia enchanted me. Whether it was fighting the White Witch with Peter, Susan, Edmund, and Lucy, sailing to the end of the world with valiant Reepicheep, or traveling across a vast, lonely moor with a gloomy Marsh-wiggle named Puddleglum, over time I began to see the deeper meanings behind the brilliant storytelling.

I read the Chronicles five times through that summer. I cried each time Aslan gave his life on the stone table for Edmund. I loved it when Aslan reappeared again, resurrected and ready to defeat his enemy. Over the years I have renewed my acquaintance with the Lion and the land of Narnia again and again, and I still cry and still love it when God triumphs. At the end of my life I want to say with the Unicorn: "I have come home at last! This is my real country! I belong here. This is the land I have been looking for all my life, though I never knew it till now. The reason why I loved the old Narnia is that it sometimes looked a little like this…come further up, come further in!"

Kim Moore
Book Editor

A Bigger Perspective

I first read The Chronicles of Narnia as an adult, but I enjoyed them the way a child does. I relished the action, excitement, and suspense of the plots. I loved the good characters, especially Lucy, Reepicheep, and Puddleglum, and detested the bad characters—the White Witch, Miraz, Gumpas, Rabadash, Shift, and Rishda Tarkaan. I found myself living in another world, a world that at times seemed more real than my everyday world. Lewis was right—fairy tales are not just for children.

What I was enjoying was the imaginativeness of Lewis's stories. The Chronicles of Narnia do a marvelous thing by showing children—and adults—the glory and power of imagination. Many children, and many adults, desire deeply that the real, ordinary world around them and their real, ordinary lives are not all there is. Lewis believed with all his heart that there *are* other worlds. And he gives us one, the world of Narnia.

Some might protest that what he gives us isn't real—it's made up of images. Lewis would reply that all experience comes to us as images, including our perceptions of the "real world." What is it, then, that makes some images real while others are imaginary? The Chronicles carry us beyond material, temporal existence to a real and lasting world of the imagination. And by making room for the imaginary, they make room for the spiritual. Yes, the Chronicles affirm, there *are* other worlds.

Lewis believed that all of us long to get out of our limited selves and narrow viewpoints, and The Chronicles of Narnia enable us to do that. They let us see through the eyes and feel with the hearts of living beings different from ourselves. Anytime we enter someone else's life and world, the experience changes us. That's true also of going to Narnia. It expands our perspectives and alters our perceptions, and when we return, we carry those larger ways of perceiving things back with us. We see new things in our world, and we see old things in fresh ways.

In *The Voyage of the Dawn Treader* Lucy finds a spell "for the refreshment of the spirit." That's what I find in The Chronicles of Narnia as a whole—an imaginary Other World full of realities that refresh my life and renew my spitit.

Peter J. Schakel
Author of *The Way into Narnia*

The Great Lion and the Grand Story

I arrived late to Narnia, but still in plenty of time for it to have a profound influence on my life.

I envy those who devoured the books as children, turning the pages expectantly to discover the adventures within. But I was nearly 20 and had already been charmed by Lewis's winsome theology in *Mere Christianity* and *The Screwtape Letters*. In fact, I delayed my reading of the Chronicles in favor of the nonfiction works. After all, I reasoned, I wanted to fill my mind with the "deep stuff" before I bothered with lightweight children's stories.

Now, some 20 years later, it strikes me that The Chronicles of Narnia might contain some of Lewis's deepest and most weighty insights into faith. Sure, they don't have the philosophical precision of *Miracles* or *The Problem of Pain*, nor do they contain the amount of practical theology we find in *Mere Christianity* or *Letters to Malcolm*. But maybe their achievement is even grander, for they helped me to *feel* and *experience* the wonder of God's Grand Story.

Though a formidable apologist for the Christian faith, Lewis knew that intellectual arguments would never be completely persuasive on their own, as they are not able to fully capture the truth about God. All our logical explanations fall short. Reason, Lewis reminded us, is the organ of truth—it is the way we come to knowledge. But imagination is the organ of meaning. It helps us make sense of reality and fully experience what truth can only point toward. Lewis understood that our hearts need to be moved as well as our brains. And nothing does that better than a well-told story.

continued >>

In Lewis's work the gospel is embodied in story, myths, analogies, and allegories in order that we may see it afresh. Is not all our thinking done primarily in images? Even the most abstract language cannot help but partake of images that we use for holding an idea in our head. We cannot, for example, speak of the glory of God without holding some sort of picture in our mind of what glory looks like. So Lewis has, throughout his books, provided us with many memorable pictures that give flesh to our theological abstractions. In the profound simplicity of The Chronicles of Narnia, the witty spiritual psychology of *The Screwtape Letters*, the allegorical tracings of his intellectual journey in *The Pilgrim's Regress*, or the deeply mythic ruminations of his Space Trilogy and *Till We Have Faces*, Lewis provides fresh glimpses of truth in unexpected places. By dressing truth in new garb he made it palatable and strikingly fresh, so readers didn't feel they were being spoon-fed theology as though it was some kind of medicine.

In speaking of his Narnia tales, Lewis wondered if, by stripping the Christian doctrines of their stained glass and Sunday school associations, he could "steal past the watchful dragons" of religiosity and dogmatism. In a sense, the Narnian tales are constructed to prepare his reader for the gospel, just as the ancient myths of dying gods prepared humanity for the time when myth became fact in the person of Jesus Christ.

Lewis understood that every story is in some sense a reflection of the Grand Story of God's pursuit of the human soul. His stories call us to make that story our own. And they do that by awakening our sense of wonder. Over and over in his books he demonstrates the ability to capture those transcendent moments when we come face-to-face with something bigger than us, a realm beyond our ordinary lives. Through the doorway of his prose we have stepped from our world into another realm, a realm suffused with a holy mystery.

In his finest moments, Lewis's writing gives us the opportunity to connect with the One who is beyond all our reason and imagining. What we experience in these moments is the sense of God breaking into our lives, not the tame and tidy God of our denominational creeds, but the God of mystery and majesty and holiness. There are passages in The Chronicles of Narnia which create a strong sense of the numinous, inviting a nearly speechless awe in the presence of the mysterious "Other."

As Dom Bede Griffiths has said:

> The figure of Aslan tells us more about how Lewis understood the nature of God than anything else he wrote. It has all the hidden power and majesty and awesomeness which Lewis associated with God, but also His glory and tenderness and even the humor which He believed belonged to Him, so that children could run up to Him and throw their arms around Him and kiss Him.

Perhaps that is why The Chronicles of Narnia move me so deeply and unexpectedly. They contain within them glimpses of transcendence, of a story bigger than first meets the eye. On initial examination they may seem simple children's tales with talking animals, witches, and young boys and girls discovering their inner strength and courage. But the reader is always aware that something magical, something supernatural, might just break through at any moment.

One can feel the breath of the great Lion rustling through the pages as the story of Lucy, Peter, Susan, and Edmund becomes your story, my story…part of the Grand Story…

Terry Glaspey
Author of *Not a Tame Lion:*
The Spiritual Legacy of C.S. Lewis

Aslan

Big lion

Very very powerful

Very very good

Gold, fast, dangerous

Talking King

Roaring

Aslan

Josh Teigen,
age 8